un in Fall

early reader

THE PUMPKIN PATCH

By Cliff Griswold

Gareth Stevens PUBLISHING

Please visit our website, www.garethstevens.com. For a free color catalog of all our high-quality books, call toll free 1-800-542-2595 or fax 1-877-542-2596.

Library of Congress Cataloging-in-Publication Data

Griswold, Cliff.
The pumpkin patch / Cliff Griswold.
pages cm. — (Fun in fall)
Includes index.
ISBN 978-1-4824-1789-0 (pbk.)
ISBN 978-1-4824-1791-3 (6 pack)
ISBN 978-1-4824-1788-3 (library binding)
1. Pumpkin—Juvenile literature. I. Title. II. Series: Griswold, Cliff. Fun in fall.
SB347.G75 2015
635'.62—dc23

2014022975

First Edition

Published in 2015 by
Gareth Stevens Publishing
111 East 14th Street, Suite 349
New York, NY 10003

Editor: Ryan Nagelhout
Designer: Nicholas Domiano

Photo credits: Cover, pp. 1, 5, 17 Andy Dean Photography/Shutterstock.com; p. 7 © iStockphoto.com/arekmalang; p. 9 Micha Rosenwirth/Shutterstock.com; p. 11 val lawless/Shutterstock.com; p. 13 Malgorzata Litkowska/Shutterstock.com; p. 15 Levranii/Shutterstock.com; p. 19 Olha Afanasieva/Shutterstock.com; pp. 21, 24 (pumpkin seeds) KellyBoreson/Shutterstock.com; pp. 23, 24 (pumpkin pie) Brent Hofacker/Shutterstock.com.

Printed in the United States of America

CPSIA compliance information: Batch #CW15GS: For further information contact Gareth Stevens, New York, New York at 1-800-542-2595.

Contents

Fall Family Fun. 4
Lots of Pumpkins. 8
Time to Eat. 18
Words to Know 24
Index. 24

My family
loves pumpkins.

We go to a farm.
They grow
pumpkins there!

Pumpkin Patch

There are
many different kinds.

Most pumpkins
are orange.

Some are white.

Pumpkins can be very small!

I picked a big pumpkin.

You can even
eat pumpkins.

My mom bakes
pumpkin seeds.

She also made us pumpkin pie!

Words to Know

pumpkin pie

pumpkin seeds

Index

farm 6
kinds 8
pie 22
seeds 20